Off the ground

S · T · E · P

Dave Boyle
Wendy Pitt

CAMBRIDGE UNIVERSITY PRESS

Published by the Press Syndicate of the University of Cambridge
The Pitt Building, Trumpington Street, Cambridge CB2 1RP
40 West 20th Street, New York, NY 10011–4211, USA
10 Stamford Road, Oakleigh, Victoria 3166, Australia

In association with Staffordshire County Council

© Cambridge University Press 1992

First published 1992

Printed in Great Britain by Scotprint Ltd, Musselburgh

Designed and produced by Gecko Limited, Bicester, Oxon.

A catalogue record of this book is available from the British Library.

ISBN 0 521 406285

PICTURE ACKNOWLEDGEMENTS

Christopher Coggins 9, 28
Robert Harding Picture Library 5tr, 5bl, 22t, 25tl, 25cl, 31c, 31r.
Images 3, 4b, 15tl, 15b, 18tr, 19br, 24t, 31t, 31bl, 32.
Last Resort 5br.
NHPA 15tr, 18bl, 25br.
Zefa Ltd. 4t, 5tl, 14, 15cl, 15cr, 19cl, 24c, 24b, 25tr, 25cr, 25bl.

Picture Research by Linda Proud

NOTICE TO TEACHERS

The contents of this book are in the copyright of Cambridge University Press. Unauthorised copying of any of the pages is not only illegal but also goes against the interests of the authors.

For authorised copying please check that your school has a licence (through the Local Education Authority) from the Copyright Licensing Agency which enables you to copy small parts of the text in limited numbers.

Contents

High tech 4

In the air 14

On the water 24

Hi-Tech

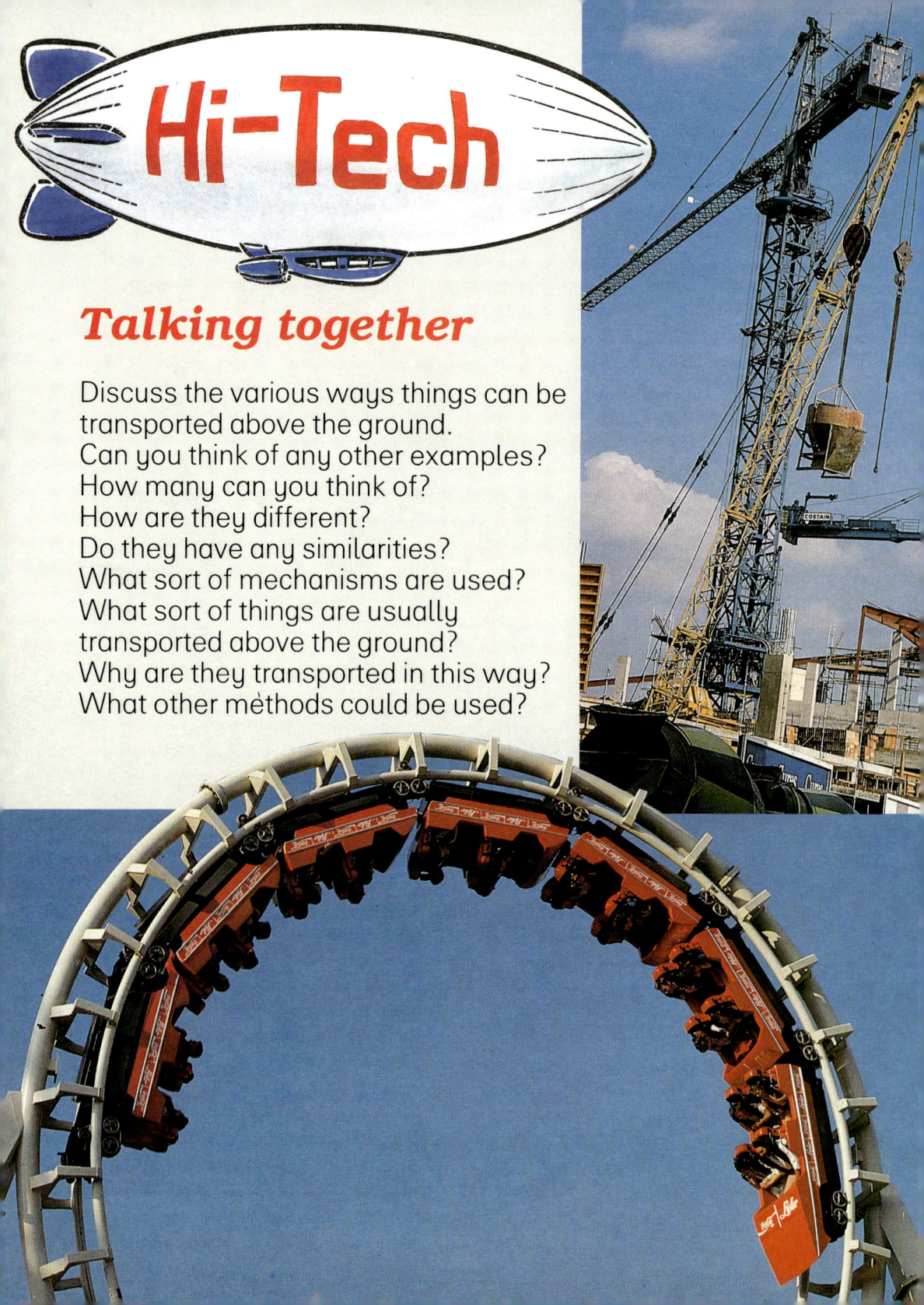

Talking together

Discuss the various ways things can be transported above the ground.
Can you think of any other examples?
How many can you think of?
How are they different?
Do they have any similarities?
What sort of mechanisms are used?
What sort of things are usually transported above the ground?
Why are they transported in this way?
What other methods could be used?

5

The need

A local toy shop wants an overhead mobile display to advertise their new toys. They have decided to ask local children to design an exciting display. The most original and interesting design will be used in the shop.

Developing your design

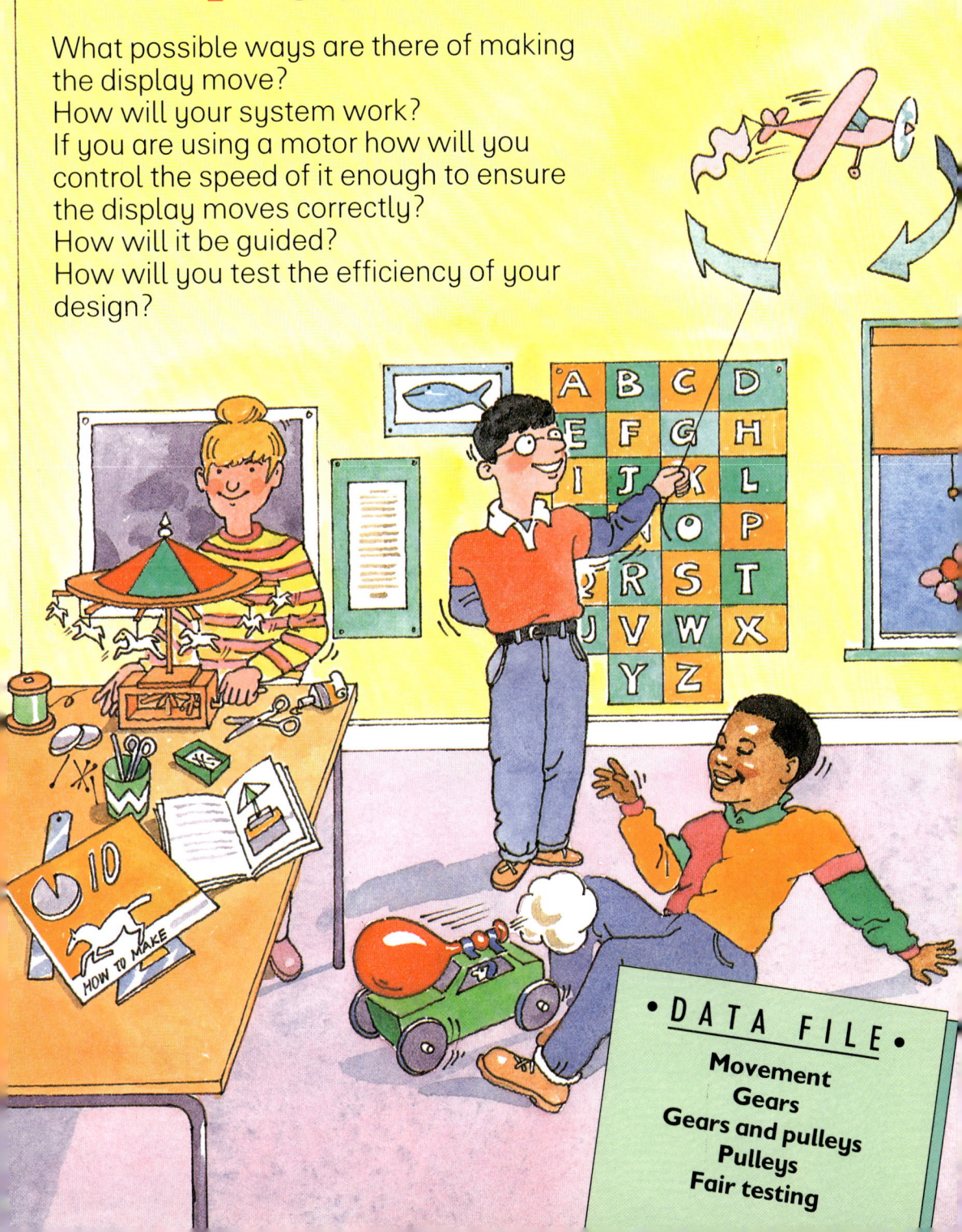

What possible ways are there of making the display move?
How will your system work?
If you are using a motor how will you control the speed of it enough to ensure the display moves correctly?
How will it be guided?
How will you test the efficiency of your design?

· DATA FILE ·
Movement
Gears
Gears and pulleys
Pulleys
Fair testing

Propulsion

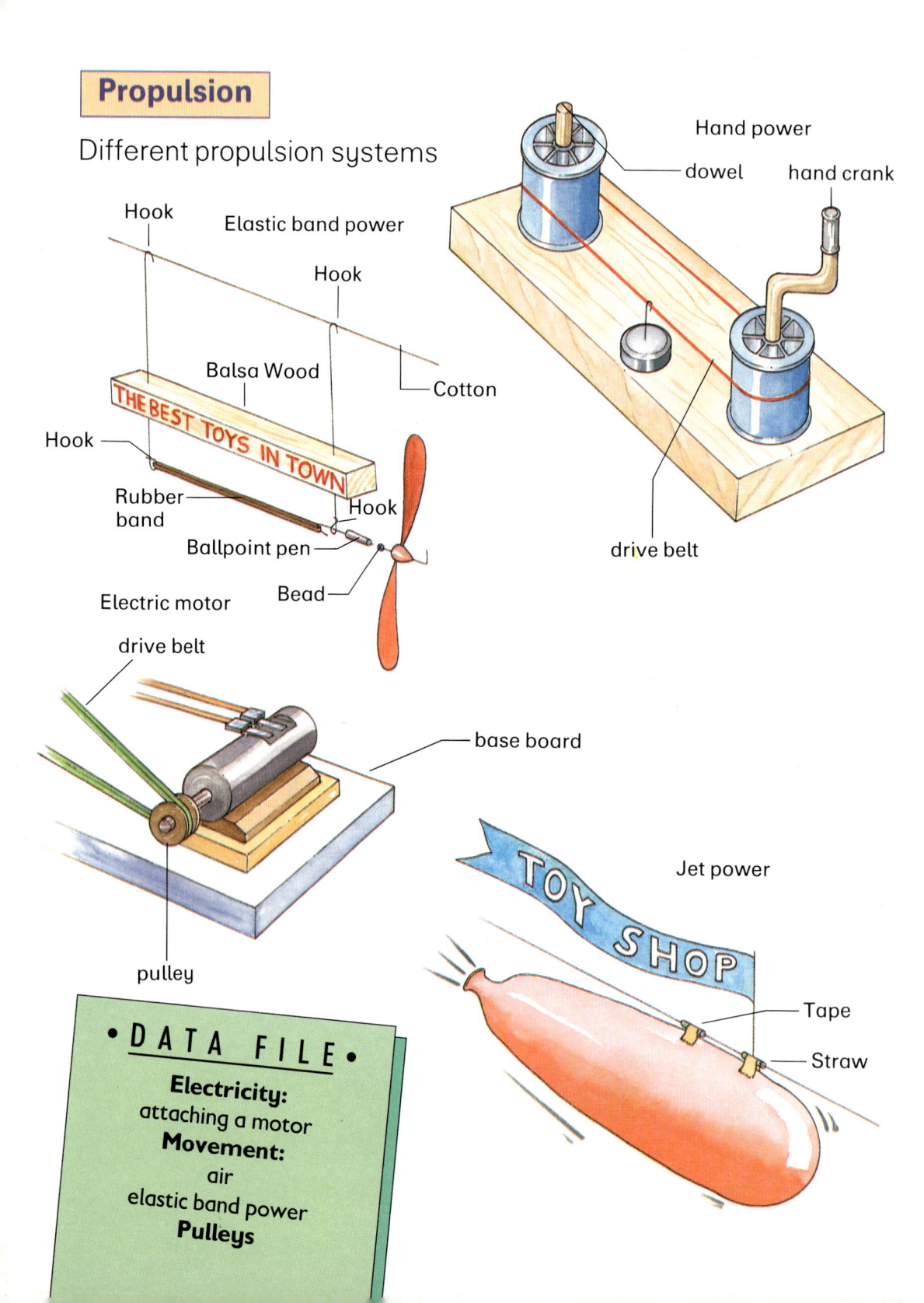

Different propulsion systems

Elastic band power

- Hook
- Hook
- Balsa Wood
- Cotton
- THE BEST TOYS IN TOWN
- Hook
- Rubber band
- Hook
- Ballpoint pen
- Bead

Hand power
- dowel
- hand crank
- drive belt

Electric motor
- drive belt
- base board
- pulley

Jet power
- TOY SHOP
- Tape
- Straw

• DATA FILE •
Electricity:
attaching a motor
Movement:
air
elastic band power
Pulleys

Control

Different switching systems

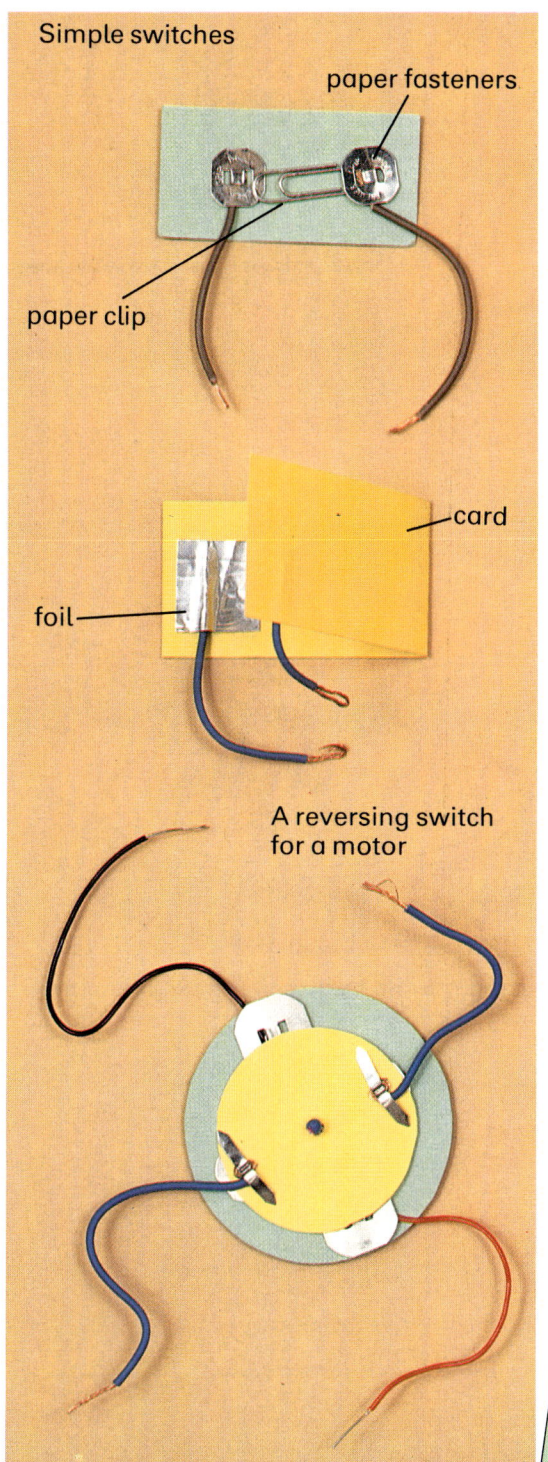

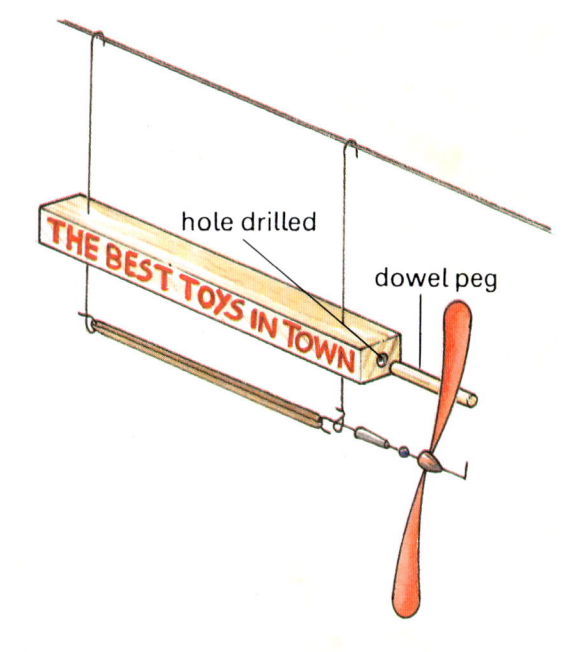

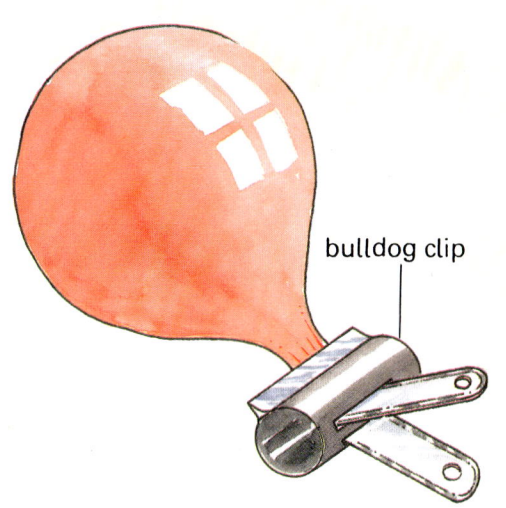

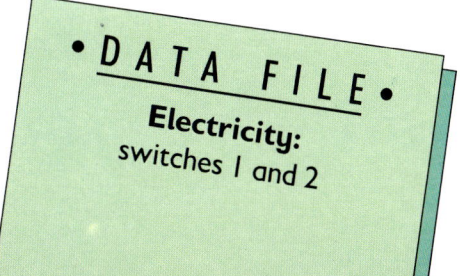

Simple switches

- paper fasteners
- paper clip
- card
- foil

A reversing switch for a motor

- hole drilled
- dowel peg
- THE BEST TOYS IN TOWN
- bulldog clip

• <u>D A T A   F I L E</u> •
Electricity:
switches 1 and 2

9

Gears

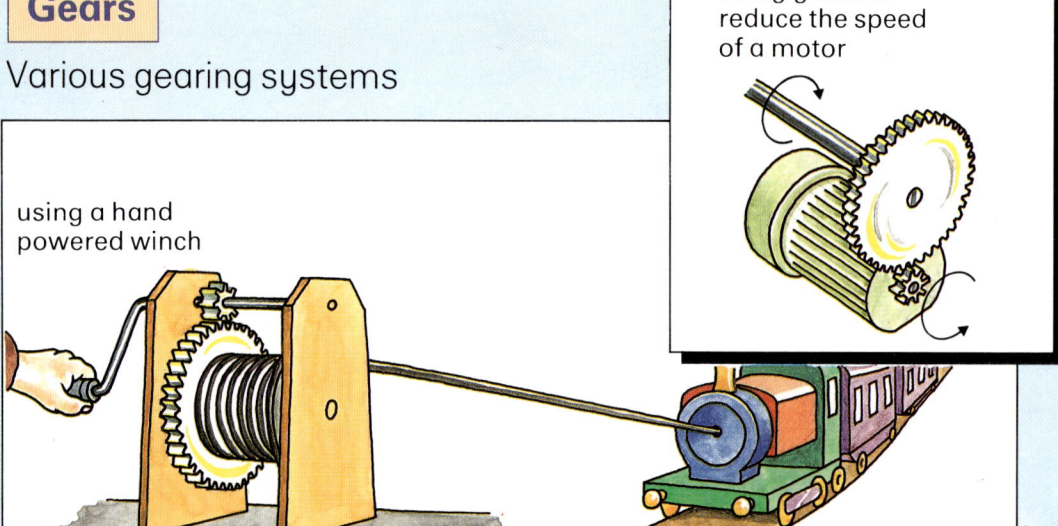

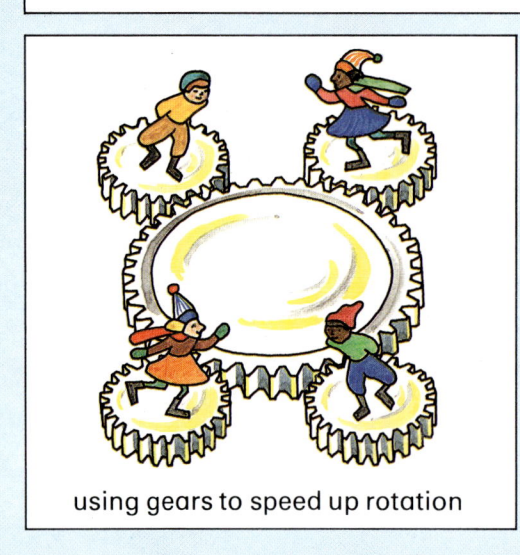

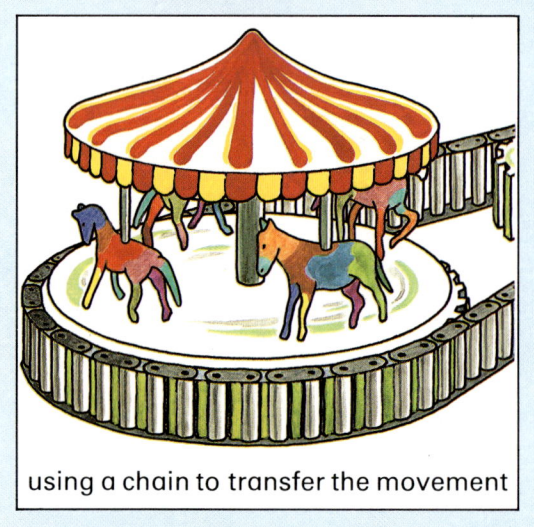

Various gearing systems

using a hand powered winch

using gears to reduce the speed of a motor

using gears to speed up rotation

using a chain to transfer the movement

• D A T A   F I L E •

Gears and pulleys
Gears:
changing speed
low cost
moving things more easily
transmitting movement

Graphic Skills

Some ways to make your display more interesting.

• D A T A   F I L E •
Graphics:
lettering 1 and 2
logos and symbols
cartoons 1 and 2

11

How could the shop be decorated?

More ideas

Design and make an overhead gantry system to lift heavy objects.

Devise a system for loading and unloading lorries.

Devise a sorting device which would automatically sort out different sized marbles for the toy shop.

13

In the Air

Talking together

How many different ways of moving through the air can you see in the pictures?
Can you think of any other ways?
What is different about them?
What is the same?
What are the main reasons for choosing these methods of transport?

15

The need

Imagine your friend is being held prisoner by a group of bandits but you have thought of a brilliant escape plan. You need to get a message to your friend without the guards seeing or hearing you. The best idea seems to be sending a message over the guards' heads and into the fenced area where your friend is being held.

Make a sketch map showing where your friend is being kept with details of where the guards are patrolling and where you will be able to launch your message and remain concealed.

Developing your design

What different methods could you use to carry the message through the air?

You could try the following ideas:

a) a stone and parachute
b) a paper aeroplane
c) a balloon
d) a spinning shape
e) a kite

Have you any other ideas which could be used?
Set up a fair test to find out which method would be the best for carrying the message.
Don't forget things like accuracy, speed and the need to remain silent and unobserved.

• DATA FILE •
Graphics:
mapping 1
mapping 2
Movement:
air 1
air 2
Fair testing

17

Try different parachute designs.

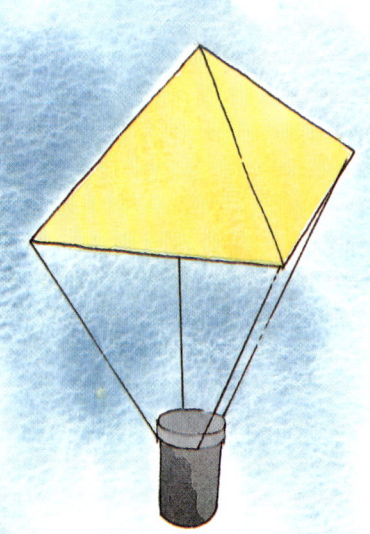

• DATA FILE •
Movement:
air 1
air 2

18

Make some paper aeroplanes.

Construct a hot air balloon.

Example 1
cut out 6 tissue paper panels

- 50 cm
- 70 cm
- 25 cm

glue together

Example 2

- 50 cm
- 50 cm
- 70 cm

Tissue Paper

HOT AIR

Thin wire frame

Thin wire ring

HOT AIR

20

Try different spinning shapes.

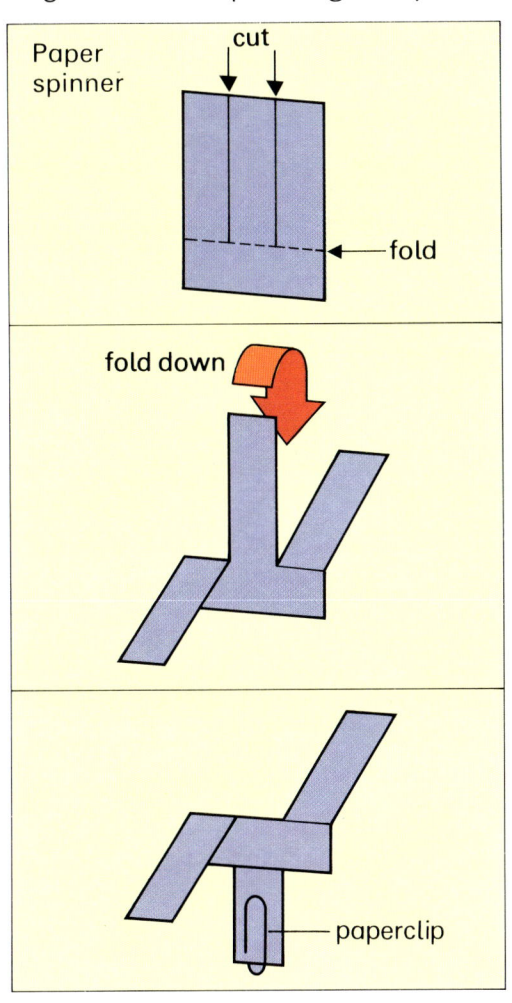

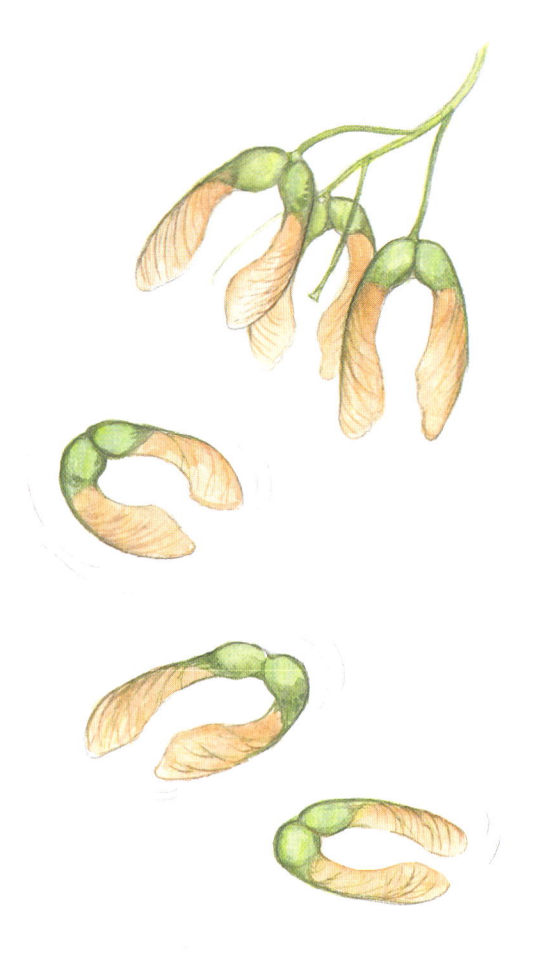

Paper spinner

cut

fold

fold down

paperclip

Flicking card shapes

Try different designs of kite.

22

More ideas

Design something which would remain airborne for the maximum possible time.
Design something which would descend slowly but accurately enough to hit a target.
Develop an airborne advertising device to promote a new product.
How could you use the wind to carry something as far as possible?

On the Water

Talking together

Here are some different methods of travelling through water.
Can you think of any other methods? What have they all got in common? What differences are there between them? Which methods of propulsion are used? Why are they shaped the way they are? How would you describe their shapes?

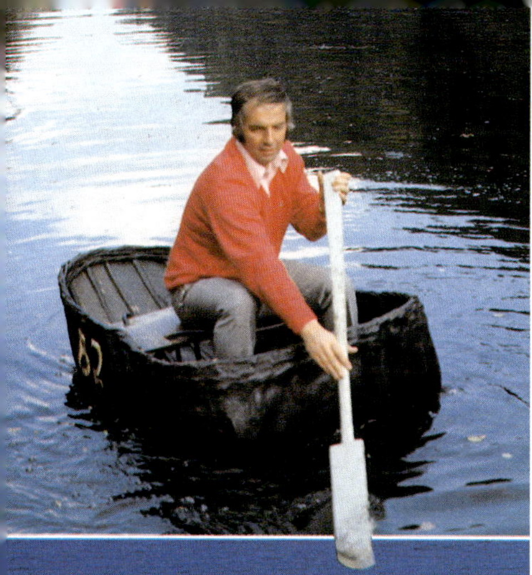

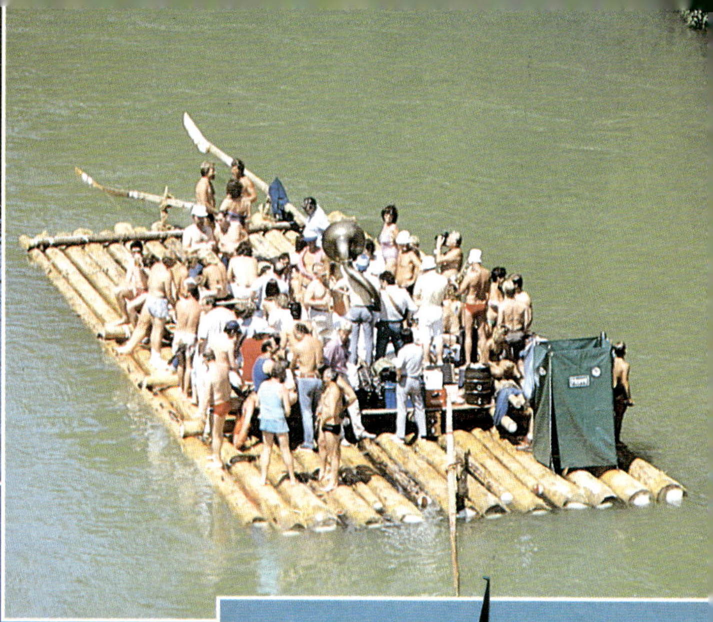

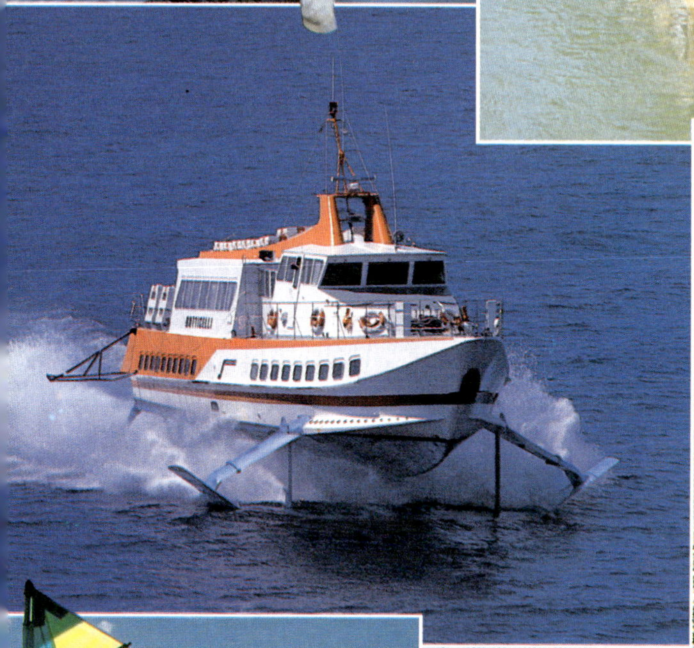

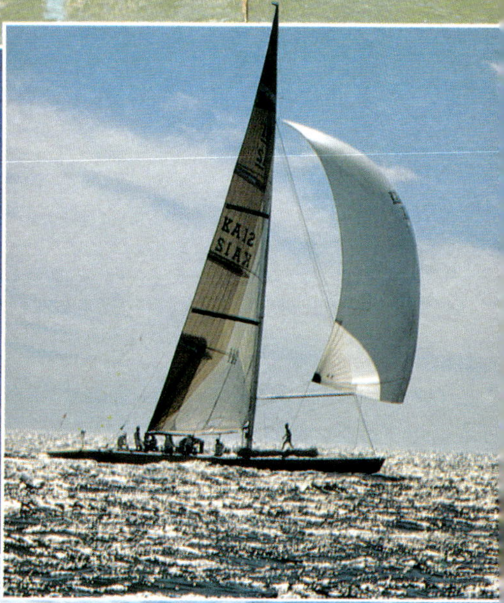

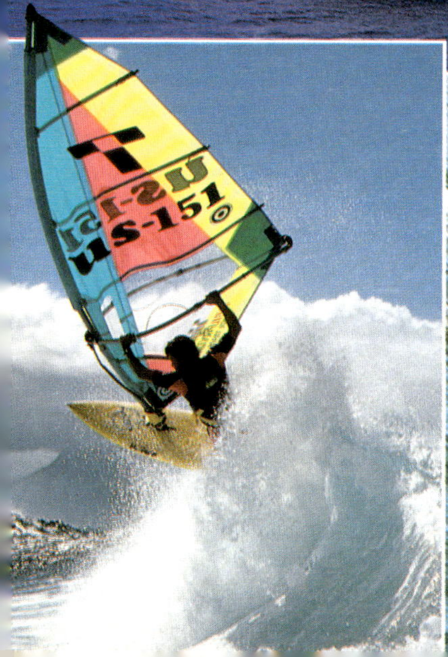
US-151

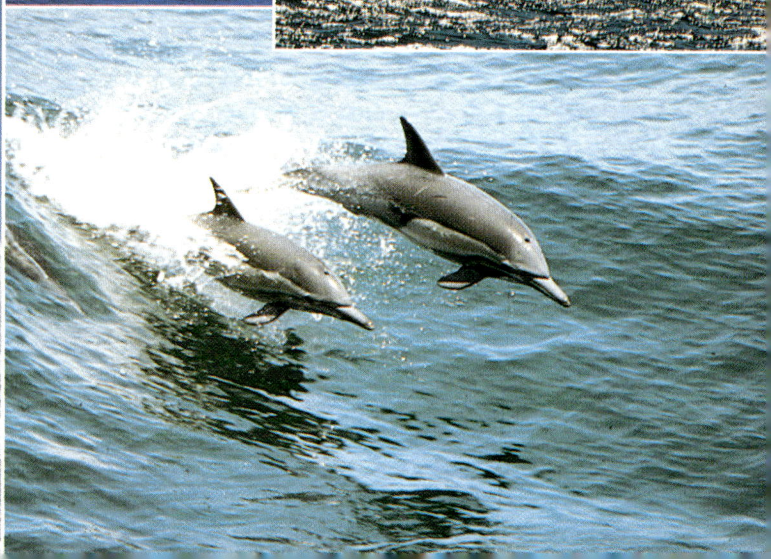

The need

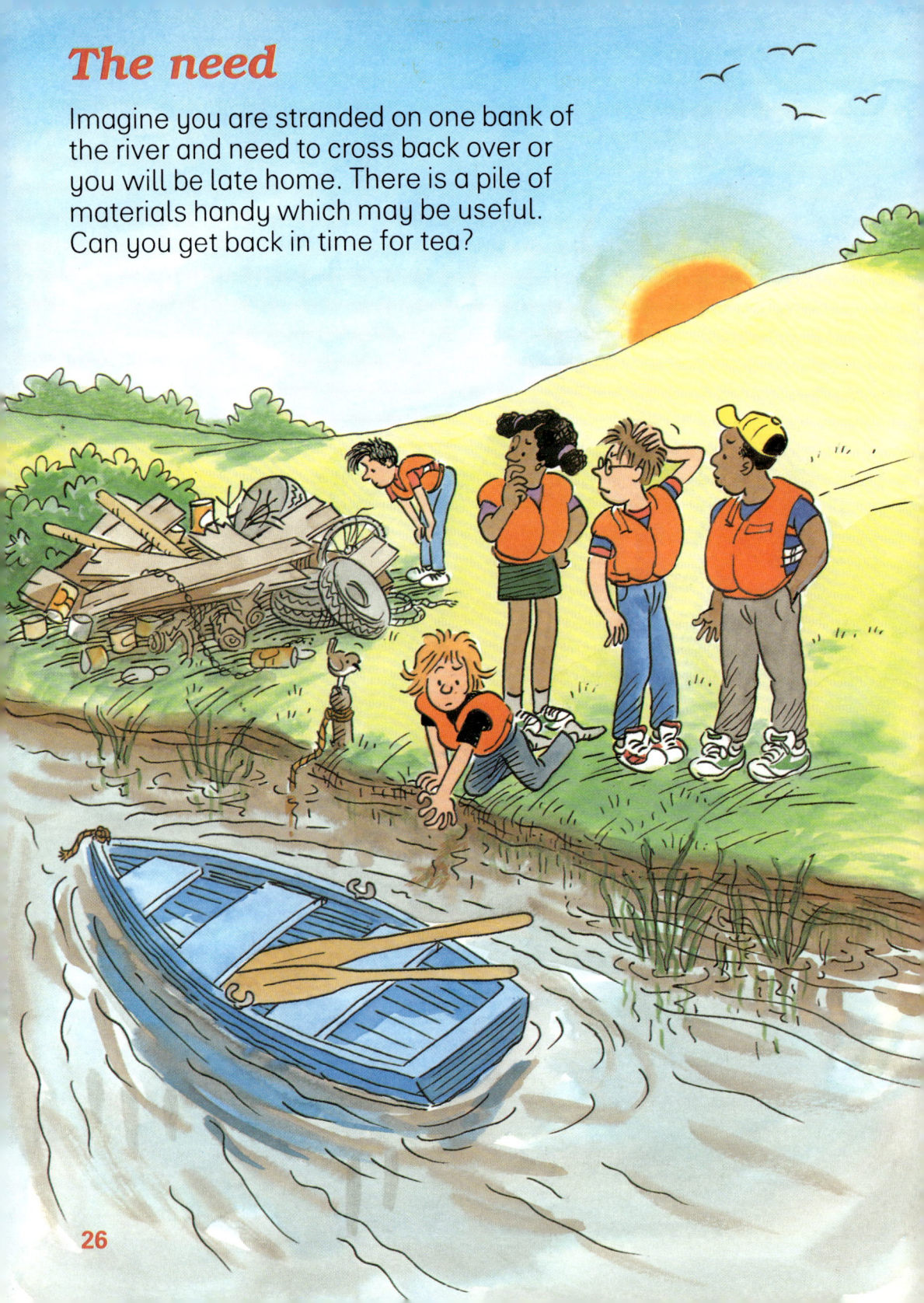

Imagine you are stranded on one bank of the river and need to cross back over or you will be late home. There is a pile of materials handy which may be useful. Can you get back in time for tea?

Developing your design

Which of the materials available will float?
Which would be most suitable to carry you back?
How will you join these materials together?
You will need to power the craft in some way otherwise you will just drift downstream.
Consider the methods of propulsion that are available:
- oars
- elastic bands
- wind power
- an electric motor
- balloon power

How will the craft be steered to ensure a safe landing on the opposite bank?
How can you be secured on the craft to ensure your safety?

• DATA FILE •
Recycling materials

27

Buoyancy

Test materials for buoyancy.

• DATA FILE •
Fair testing

Joining materials

Join materials in different ways.

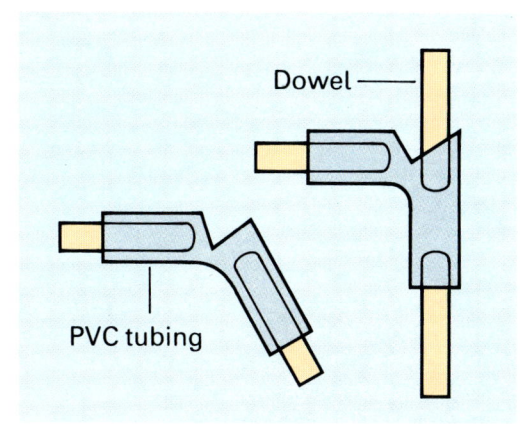

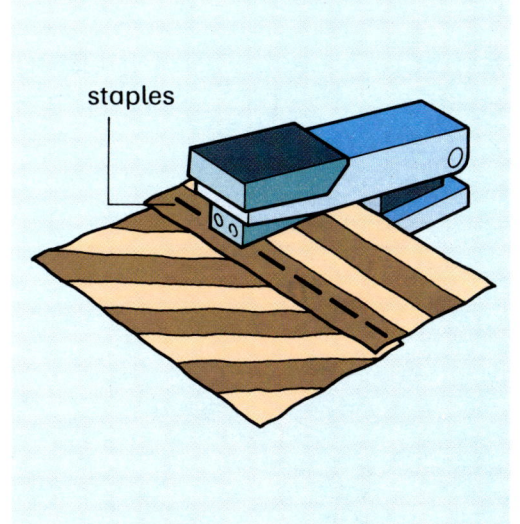

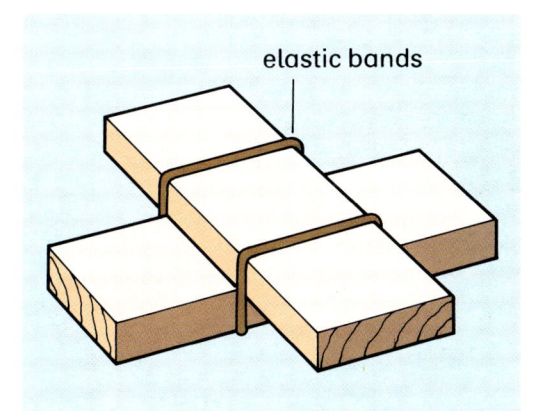

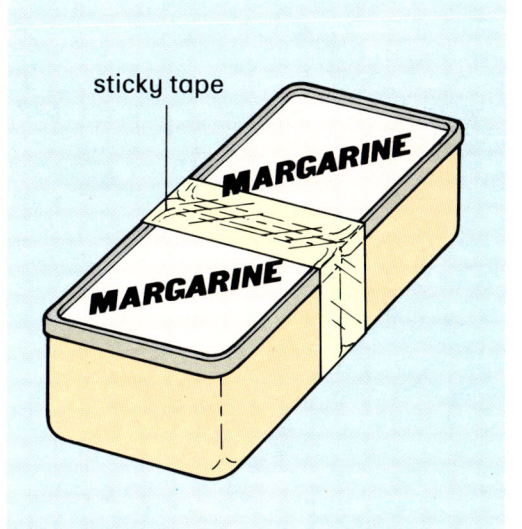

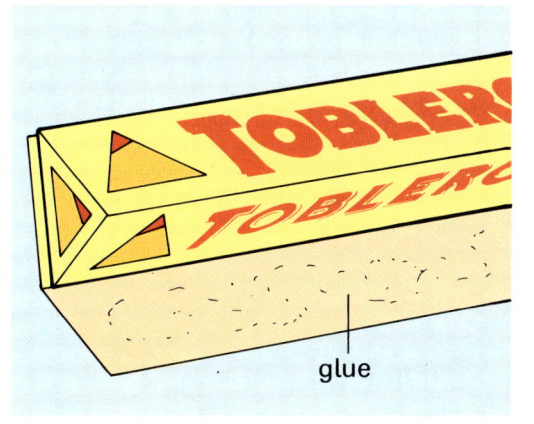

Dowel

PVC tubing

staples

elastic bands

sticky tape

MARGARINE

glue

• D A T A F I L E •
**Recycling materials
Wood:**
quick joining methods

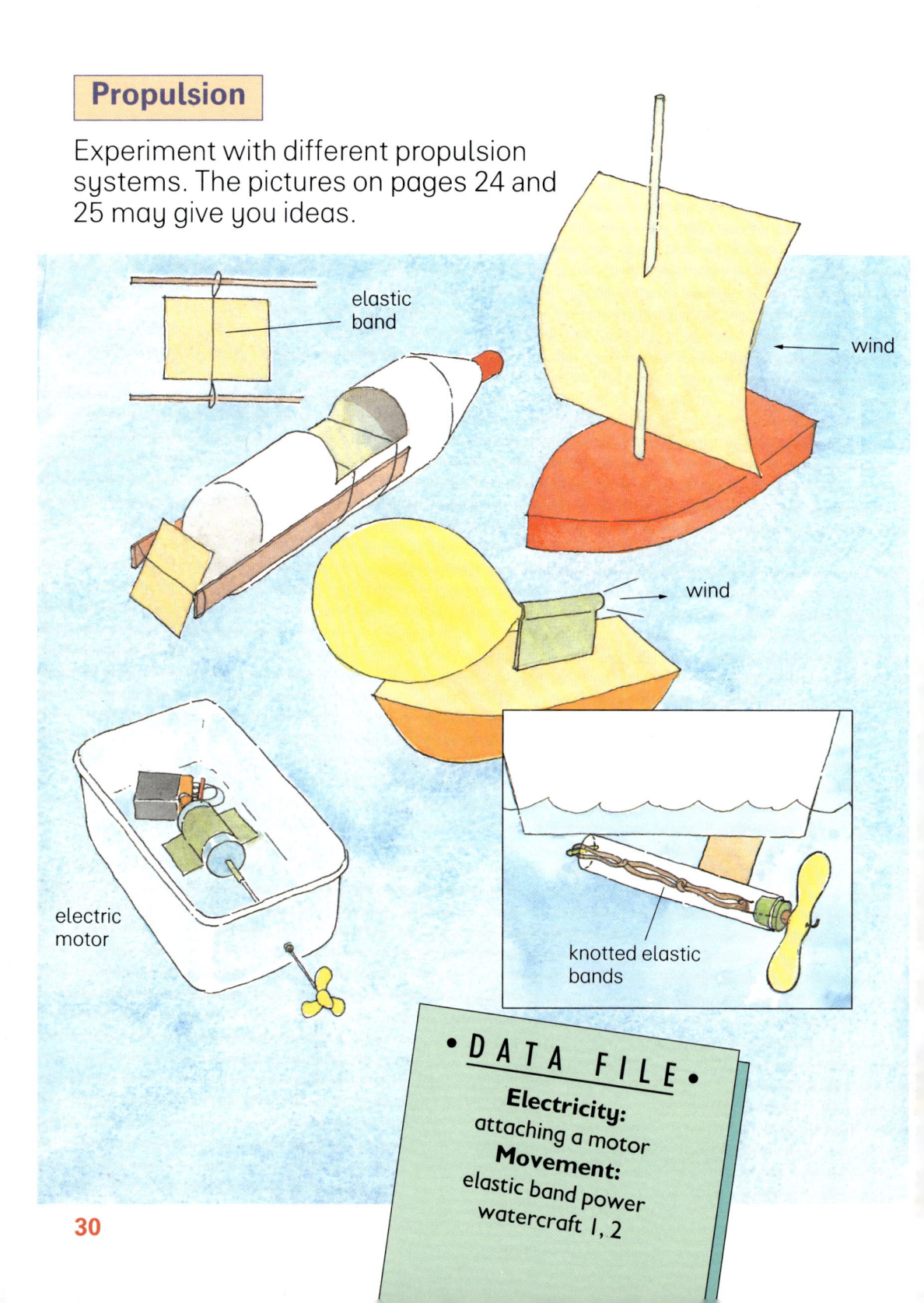

Propulsion

Experiment with different propulsion systems. The pictures on pages 24 and 25 may give you ideas.

elastic band

wind

wind

electric motor

knotted elastic bands

• **DATA FILE** •
Electricity:
attaching a motor
Movement:
elastic band power
watercraft 1, 2

30

Steering

Experiment with different steering systems.

balloon

DATA FILE

Movement:
watercraft 1, 2

More ideas

Design some buoyancy aids in case of accident.

Develop a design for a submersible craft which could be used to explore the river bed.

Design a poster to promote water safety.

Develop a board game promoting water safety.